Help your child press out the stickers and place them on the correct pages.

ag

ine

an

ap

ar

at

en

et

ig

in

op

ot

ow

ub

ug

ail

ake   all   ate

eep   eet   ell

est   ick   ing

ink   ock   ook

own   ark

 own

art

ark

My Phonics WORD BOOK

Written by Cass Hollander
Illustrated by Dick Morgado

Published by McClanahan Book Co., Inc. 23 West 26th St.
New York, NY 10010
Printed in the U.S.A.

ag

bag
drag
flag
rag
tag
wag

bag

Pack a **bag.**

rag

Use a **rag.**

drag

Drag a bag.

tag

Playing **tag**

flag

Wave a **flag.**

wag

Tails that **wag**

am

clam
dam
ham
jam
slam
yam

clam

Dig a **clam.**

jam

Mmmm…mmm **jam**

dam

Make a **dam.**

slam

Don't let it **slam!**

ham

Bake a **ham.**

yam

Pick a **yam.**

an

can
fan
man
pan
ran
van

can

Open a **can.**

pan

Wash a **pan.**

fan

Stop that **fan!**

ran

She ran and **ran.**

man

Meet a **man.**

van

I have a **van.**

ap

cap
clap
lap
map
nap
strap

cap

I love my **cap!**

map

Look at the **map.**

clap

Tap and **clap.**

nap

Take a **nap.**

lap

Sit on a **lap.**

strap

Fix the **strap.**

ar

bar
car
far
jar
star
tar

bar

Chocolate **bar**

jar

Pickle **jar**

car

Yellow **car**

star

Wish on a **star.**

far

Going **far**

tar

Stuck in **tar.**

at

bat
cat
fat
hat
mat
sat

bat

Swing a **bat.**

hat

Hold on to your **hat!**

cat

Pet a **cat.**

mat

Sweep the **mat.**

fat

Short and **fat**

sat

The cat just **sat.**

en

hen
men
pen
ten
then
when

hen

Get that **hen!**

ten

Count to **ten.**

men

Ten **men**

then

Now and **then**

pen

Pick a **pen.**

when

Say **when!**

et

get
jet
let
net
pet
wet

get

Get ready! **Get** set!

net

Jump the **net.**

jet

Fly a **jet.**

pet

Feed a **pet.**

let

Let me pet.

wet

Don't get **wet!**

ig

big
dig
jig
pig
twig
wig

big

So **big!**

pig

A pretty **pig!**

dig

Dig and **dig.**

twig

Use a **twig.**

jig

Dance a **jig.**

wig

What a **wig!**

in

chin
fin
pin
spin
twin
win

chin

My **chin chin chin**

spin

Tops **spin.**

fin

A purple **fin**

twin

Find the **twin.**

pin

Find a **pin.**

win

Who will **win?**

op

chop
hop
mop
pop
stop
top

chop

Chop, chop, chop!

pop

Pop!

hop

Hop, hop, hop!

stop

I can't **stop!**

mop

Dance with a **mop.**

top

Spin a **top.**

got

What have you **got?**

not

Ready or **not!**

hot

Too **hot!**

pot

Oh no! The **pot!**

lot

Thanks a **lot!**

spot

A bad **spot**

OW

bow
chow
cow
how
now
plow

bow

Take a **bow.**

how

Find out **how.**

chow

Time for **chow!**

now

Come out **now!**

cow

Milk a **cow.**

plow

Pull a **plow.**

ub

club
cub
rub
scrub
shrub
tub

club

Be in the **club!**

scrub

Scrub and **scrub.**

cub

Hug a **cub.**

shrub

Plant a **shrub.**

rub

Pat. Don't **rub.**

tub

Duck in the **tub.**

ug

bug
hug
jug
mug
rug
tug

bug

See a **bug.**

mug

This is my **mug.**

hug

A big **hug!**

rug

Sweep the **rug.**

jug

Fill the **jug.**

tug

Tug and **tug**

ail

mail
nail
pail
sail
snail
tail

mail

Get the **mail.**

sail

Put up the **sail.**

nail

Hammer a **nail.**

snail

Race a **snail.**

pail

Fill a **pail.**

tail

Wag a **tail.**

ain

brain
chain
plain
rain
stain
train

TOY SALE

brain

Use your **brain.**

rain

Rain, rain, rain!

chain

Make a **chain.**

stain

Fix a **stain.**

plain

Fancy or **plain?**

train

Take a **train.**

ake

bake
cake
lake
rake
snake
take

bake

Time to **bake.**

rake

Drop the **rake.**

cake

I love **cake!**

snake

Oh, oh! A **snake!**

lake

Jump in the **lake.**

take

Take the cake.

all

ball
call
fall
hall
small
wall

ball

Play **ball.**

hall

Hide in the **hall.**

call

Make a **call.**

small

Make yourself **small.**

fall

Do not **fall.**

wall

Paint a **wall.**

ate

date
gate
late
plate
skate
state

date

What is the **date?**

plate

Dropped a **plate!**

gate

Open the **gate.**

skate

Fix a **skate.**

late

Too **late!**

state

Find your **state.**

- 42 -

creep

Caterpillars **creep.**

keep

Sell or **keep?**

deep

Dive down **deep.**

sheep

Counting **sheep**

jeep

Go in a **jeep.**

sleep

Go to **sleep.**

eet

beet
feet
greet
meet
sheet
street

BEETS

beet

Pull up a **beet.**

meet

Did you **meet?**

feet

Tap your **feet.**

sheet

Fold a **sheet.**

greet

Meet and **greet.**

street

Cross a **street.**

ell

bell
fell
shell
smell
tell
well

bell

Ring the **bell.**

smell

What a **smell!**

fell

Who **fell?**

tell

Show and **tell.**

shell

Hide in your **shell.**

well

Go to the **well.**

est

best
nest
pest
rest
test
vest

best

Do your **best.**

rest

Sit and **rest.**

nest

Make a **nest.**

test

Take a **test.**

pest

What a **pest!**

vest

Button your **vest.**

ick

brick
chick
kick
lick
sick
stick

brick

Lay a **brick.**

lick

Lick and **lick!**

chick

A baby **chick**

sick

I feel **sick.**

kick

Make the **kick.**

stick

Get a **stick.**

ing

king
ring
sing
sting
string
swing

king

Meet a **king.**

sting

Bees can **sting!**

ring

Look at my **ring.**

string

Too much **string!**

sing

Dance and **sing.**

swing

Swing on a **swing.**

ink

drink
pink
rink
sink
think
wink

drink

Take a **drink.**

sink

Dishes in the **sink**

pink

Paint it **pink.**

think

Sit and **think.**

rink

Skate in the **rink.**

wink

Smile and **wink.**

ock

block
clock
dock
lock
rock
sock

block

Add a **block.**

lock

Open the **lock.**

clock

Set the **clock.**

rock

Find a **rock.**

dock

Step on the **dock.**

sock

Oh, no! My **sock!**

ook

book
brook
cook
hook
look
shook

book

I like my **book.**

hook

Use the **hook!**

brook

Fall in the **brook.**

look

Take a **look.**

cook

Cook, cook, cook!

shook

He **shook** and **shook!**

own

brown
clown
crown
down
frown
town

brown

Chocolate is **brown.**

down

Don't look **down!**

clown

Dance with a **clown.**

frown

Smile! Don't **frown!**

crown

Put on a **crown.**

town

Go to **town.**

ark

bark
dark
mark
park
shark
spark

art

cart
dart
part
smart
start
tart

TARTS

bark

They all **bark!**

park

In the **park**

dark

It's very **dark.**

shark

Meet a **shark.**

mark

Make a **mark.**

spark

See a **spark.**

cart

Push a **cart.**

tart

Eat a **tart.**

dart

Look out for the **dart.**

smart

Get **smart.**

part

Play a **part.**

start

When does it **start?**

Phonogram stickers
Help your child
press out the stickers
and place them on
the correct pages.

ip

it

ear

y

ad

ow

eat

aw

ut

ice

ay

ack

ill

ed

and

ay

y

ive unk ole
old eel ool
one ike ose
orn oat ound
ump oil unch

ose   ound   unch

ice

ill

ine

old

one

ive

orn

ump

unk

eel

ike

oil

oat

ool

ole

My Phonics
WORD BOOK II

Written by Cass Hollander
Illustrated by Polly Jordan

y

cry
dry
fly
sky
spy
try

2

cry

Don't **cry**.

sky

Blue as the **sky**

dry

Wash or **dry**?

spy

I **spy**.

fly

Fly away, **fly**!

try

Give it a **try**.

ad

bad
Dad
glad
mad
pad
sad

bad

Too **bad!**

mad

Don't get **mad.**

Dad

Dear old **Dad!**

pad

Grab a **pad.**

glad

Feeling **glad**

sad

So **sad**

aw

draw
law
paw
raw
saw
straw

draw

Color and **draw**.

raw

Eat carrots **raw**.

law

It's the **law**.

saw

Who saw my **saw**?

paw

Shake a **paw**.

straw

Drink with a **straw**.

ay

clay
day
play
say
tray
way

clay

Play with **clay**.

say

What did you **say?**

day

What a great **day!**

tray

Take a **tray**.

play

Come out and **play!**

way

Which **way?**

ed

bed
fed
red
shed
sled
Ted

10

bed

Time for **bed**.

shed

A garden **shed**

fed

Has the dog been **fed?**

sled

What a fast **sled**!

red

My nose is **red**!

Ted

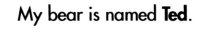

My bear is named **Ted**.

ip

chip
flip
ship
sip
trip
zip

chip

Eat a **chip**.

sip

Take a **sip**.

flip

Do a **flip**.

trip

Go on a **trip**.

ship

See a **ship**.

zip

Button or **zip**?

it

fit
hit
kit
pit
quit
sit

fit

Does it **fit**?

pit

Peach **pit**

hit

It's a **hit**!

quit

Time to **quit**.

kit

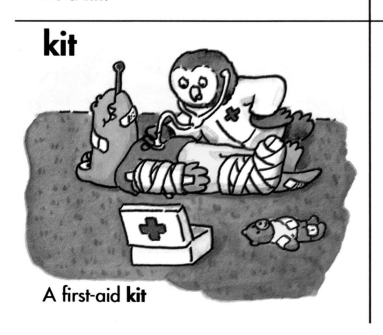

A first-aid **kit**

sit

A place to **sit**

OW

blow
grow
low
row
snow
throw

blow

Blow, wind, **blow**!

row

Ducks in a **row**

grow

Flowers **grow**.

snow

Let it **snow**!

low

Get down **low**.

throw

What a **throw**!

ut

but
cut
nut
rut
shut
strut

but

I like it, **but** . . .

rut

In a **rut**

cut

Scissors **cut**.

shut

Open and **shut**.

nut

Have a **nut**.

strut

Roosters **strut**.

ack

back
crack
pack
quack
snack
track

back

Come **back**!

quack

Ducks **quack**.

crack

Step on a **crack**!

snack

Fix a **snack**.

pack

Time to **pack**.

track

Train on the **track**

and

band
grand
hand
land
sand
stand

band

Here comes the **band**!

land

Where can I **land**?

grand

The music is **grand**!

sand

Castles of **sand**

hand

Hand in **hand**

stand

Sit or **stand**?

ave

brave
cave
gave
save
shave
wave

24

brave

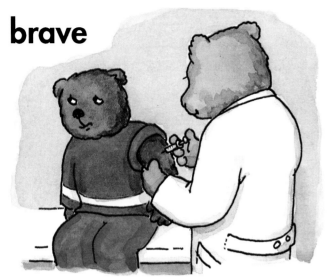

Be **brave**.

save

Save, save, save!

cave

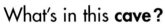

What's in this **cave**?

shave

Get a **shave**.

gave

Look what he **gave**.

wave

Smile and **wave**.

ear

clear
dear
ear
hear
near
tear

clear

Water is **clear**.

hear

Did you **hear**?

dear

Letters start with **Dear**.

near

Far and **near**

ear

Scratch an **ear**.

tear

Shed a **tear**.

eat

beat
meat
neat
seat
treat
wheat

beat

Beat, beat, beat!

seat

Take a **seat**.

meat

Cut the **meat**.

treat

Trick or **treat**?

neat

Nice and **neat**

wheat

White or **wheat**?

ice

dice
ice
mice
nice
slice
twice

30

dice

Roll the **dice**.

nice

Very **nice**

ice

Skate on **ice**.

slice

Have a **slice**.

mice

Three blind **mice**

twice

Mice **twice**!

ill

bill
chill
grill
hill
spill
still

bill

Pay the **bill**.

hill

Climb the **hill**.

chill

Feel a **chill**.

spill

Don't **spill**!

grill

Hot off the **grill**

still

Stand **still**.

ine

fine
line
mine
nine
pine
shine

34

fine

Feeling **fine**

nine

1, 2, 3, 4, 5, 6, 7, 8, 9

Count to **nine**.

line

Stand in **line**.

pine

Which is **pine**?

mine

Mine, all **mine**!

shine

See them **shine**!

ive

alive
dive
drive
five
hive
jive

36

alive

It's **alive**!

five

Room for **five**?

dive

Take a **dive**.

hive

Bees in a **hive**

drive

Go for a **drive**.

jive

Jump and **jive**.

old

cold
fold
gold
hold
old
told

cold

Brrrr . . . It's **cold**!

hold

A hand to **hold**

fold

Wash and **fold**.

old

How **old**?

gold

A crown of **gold**

told

Our story is **told**.

one

alone
bone
cone
phone
stone
tone

alone

All **alone**

phone

Answer the **phone**.

bone

Give a dog a **bone**.

stone

Step on a **stone**.

cone

Ice cream **cone**

tone

A nice **tone**

orn

born
corn
horn
thorn
torn
worn

born

When were you **born**?

thorn

Ouch! A **thorn**!

corn

Mmmm . . . fresh **corn**!

torn

This page is **torn**.

horn

Blow your **horn**!

worn

My shoes are **worn**.

ump

bump
dump
jump
plump
pump
stump

44

bump

What a bad **bump**!

plump

Nice and **plump**

dump

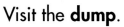

Visit the **dump**.

pump

Work the **pump**.

jump

Jump . . . jump . . . jump!

stump

Jump over the **stump**!

unk

bunk
chunk
dunk
junk
skunk
trunk

bunk

Take the top **bunk**.

junk

What *is* all this **junk**?

chunk

Have a **chunk**.

skunk

Oh, no! A **skunk**!

dunk

Cookies to **dunk**

trunk

An elephant's **trunk**

eel

feel
heel
kneel
peel
steel
wheel

48

feel

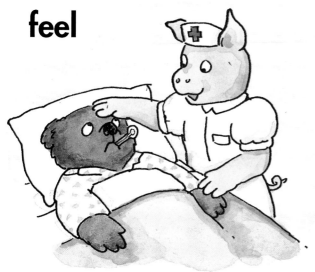

How do you **feel**?

peel

A banana **peel**

heel

Such a high **heel**!

steel

Strong as **steel**

kneel

Always **kneel**.

wheel

Turn the **wheel**!

ike

alike
bike
hike
like
spike
strike

50

alike

Dressed **alike**

like

What I **like**!

bike

Ride a **bike**.

spike

Hit a **spike**.

hike

Take a **hike**.

strike

It's a **strike**!

oat

boat
coat
float
goat
moat
throat

boat

Row the **boat**.

goat

Feed a **goat**.

coat

Button your **coat**.

moat

Fill the **moat**.

float

Will it **float**?

throat

Sore **throat**

oil

boil
broil
foil
oil
soil
spoil

boil

When will it **boil**?

oil

The car needs **oil**.

broil

Burgers to **broil**

soil

Dig in the **soil**.

foil

Wrap it in **foil**.

spoil

Milk can **spoil**.

ole

hole
mole
pole
role
sole
stole

hole

Dig a **hole**.

role

Playing a **role**

mole

It's a **mole**!

sole

A flapping **sole**

pole

Flag on a **pole**

stole

Guess what they **stole**?

ool

cool
fool
pool
school
stool
tool

58

cool

Too **cool**!

school

Go to **school**.

fool

Act like a **fool**.

stool

Sit on a **stool**.

pool

Jump in the **pool**!

tool

Use a **tool**.

ose

close
hose
nose
pose
rose
those

close

Open or **close**?

pose

Strike a **pose**.

hose

Garden **hose**

rose

Smell a **rose**.

nose

Funny **nose**

those

These or **those**?

ound

found
ground
hound
pound
round
sound

unch

bunch
crunch
hunch
lunch
munch
punch

found

Look what I **found**!

pound

Pound, pound, pound!

ground

Sit on the **ground**.

round

Bubbles are **round**.

hound

Stop that **hound**!

sound

Don't make a **sound**!

bunch

A silly **bunch**!

lunch

Stop for **lunch**.

crunch

Carrots **crunch**.

munch

Good to **munch**

hunch

Have a **hunch**.

punch

Make some **punch**.